STARTING DESIGN & TECHNOLOGY

MECHANISMS

VIJAY OZA AND MARTIN CHANDLER

Series editor: John Cave

Cassell Publishers Limited
Artillery House
Artillery Row
London SW1P 1RT

First published 1990

British Library Cataloguing in Publication Data
Oza, Vijay, *1957–*
 Mechanisms.
 1. Mechanisms
 I. Title II. Chandler, Martin III. Series
 621.8

 ISBN 0-304-31649-0

Typeset by Fakenham Photosetting Limited, Fakenham,
Norfolk

Printed and bound in Great Britain by The Bath Press, Avon

Contents

Introduction

Machines and mechanisms have been explored by people from the very beginning. They have evolved through needs, and from these needs basic principles have been derived. This book will show the importance of machines and mechanisms to our way of life. We may live in an electronic age but we still need mechanical devices to do the physical work.

The book is divided into five sections which extend the principles of mechanisms from simple to complex through everyday situations. The first section (**What Is a Machine?**) is an introduction to the vast range of everyday machines using simple concepts. The following four sections deal with situations in which we use a variety of machines to help us (**Helping Hand**), to move things (**Movement**), to measure (**Measurement**), and to control (**Control**). To help you understand and explore, there are over 40 tasks which question your knowledge of mechanisms. Those should be tackled in the context of project work.

When you come across an important word for the first time, it will be printed in **bold** letters. Try to remember these words and what they mean.

At the back of the book there is a mini-dictionary which explains the meaning of words that you may not have come across before. If you are not sure of a word, *look it up*.

1 What Is a Machine?

The Key ...

Keys have quite a long history. Examples from excavations show that keys have been used for hundreds of years. Yet if you compare these keys with modern keys they have hardly changed at all. With so many inventions and so much development over the centuries, why is it that the key has not been 'improved'? We are not, at the moment, concerned with how the lock works but with the shape of the key itself.

A mortice key

This part operates the lock mechanism.

This part is turned by finger and thumb.

One answer to why the shape of the key has remained the same for so long is that it is a simple machine that works well, so there is no need to change it.

These teeth operate the lock mechanism.

A yale key

Could you make a lock work with the keys shown below?

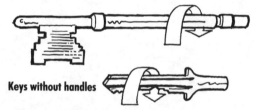

Keys without handles

How easy is it to turn these keys?

The reason that keys have a larger end is to give more leverage.

Look at the keys end on.

The older keys were much larger. Can you suggest reasons for this?

Come back to this page after you have learnt about **levers** and try to identify the type of lever used and the forces involved.

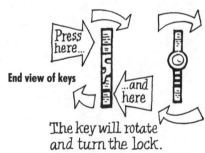

Press here...

...and here

End view of keys

The key will rotate and turn the lock.

... and Sauce Bottle

The screwtop does not have such a long history as the key, but let us ask, why is it used, and so frequently?

The main answer is that the screwtop makes an airtight seal.

When screwed on tightly, the inside of the top presses against the top of the bottle, thus keeping the contents fresh.

But why the screwtop?

This is a simple machine that works well, so it has been adapted for many uses.

The top of a sauce bottle showing a large screw-thread.

When it is first placed on to the bottle the top is loose. As you turn the top the **screw-thread** on the bottle comes into contact with two bumps on the inside of the top. As you continue to turn, the bumps are pulled down by the slope on the thread. The more you turn, the more the top is pulled down, and the better the seal.

Bump inside top

Cross section of the top of the sauce bottle with the cap.

If you just pressed down do you think you could make the same seal? The reason for using the screw-thread is because you gain a mechanical advantage.

If you rotate the top by half a turn it will only move down or up a small amount. So the force that we use to turn the top is magnified to give a greater downward force.

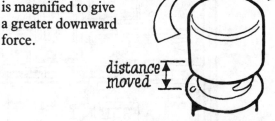

half turn

distance moved

The lid turns to close the bottle.

This will be explained in more detail in the next few pages.

Task

Can you think of other objects that use the **screw-thread**?

7

What Is a Machine?

Where Are the Machines?

Is there a definition of a machine?

How about . . . . almost anything manufactured to do a job is a machine, so anything from a supersonic plane to a nutcracker could be a machine.

We are surrounded by machines. They help us to do a variety of jobs and functions as a society. We have machines which move people and heavy objects, machines which build and destroy and, most importantly, machines which do whatever we want them to do.

The truth is that it is very difficult to avoid labelling every device as a machine.

Are machines everywhere?

We are so used to making our lives easy that we forget how many types of machines we use daily.

Do you realize how many machines are used in your home in the short space of time between when you get up and when you leave for school?

Imagine now, if you can, all the different types of machines used on a farm, in a factory, on a building site, in an office, in a school, on the roads, on the railways, in hospitals. The list is endless.

We soon discover that we cannot live without machines.

A cross-section of a house showing the variety of everyday machines.

Is It a Tool, an Instrument or a Machine?

There are numerous devices that we use every day which employ simple mechanical principles. Over the centuries of their development they have been given a variety of labels – a tool, an instrument, a machine.

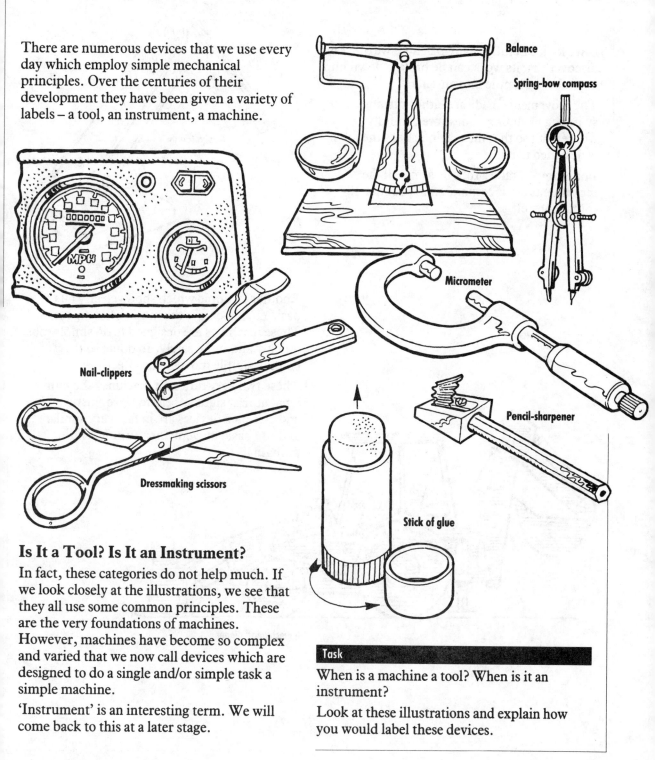

Balance

Spring-bow compass

Micrometer

Nail-clippers

Dressmaking scissors

Stick of glue

Pencil-sharpener

Is It a Tool? Is It an Instrument?

In fact, these categories do not help much. If we look closely at the illustrations, we see that they all use some common principles. These are the very foundations of machines. However, machines have become so complex and varied that we now call devices which are designed to do a single and/or simple task a simple machine.

'Instrument' is an interesting term. We will come back to this at a later stage.

Task

When is a machine a tool? When is it an instrument?

Look at these illustrations and explain how you would label these devices.

What Is a Machine?

Machines Simplified

If we look carefully at any machine we quickly discover that its work can be broken down into a number of simple **movements**.

The movements made are either turning, swinging or sliding. These are carefully worked out so that the machine does the job it is designed to do.

For example, take a robotic arm. All the movements are incorporated to produce all-round control.

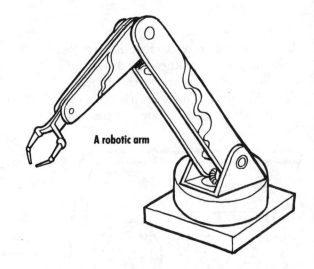

A robotic arm

Another example which shows clearly all the basic movements is the mechanical digger. These machines are designed to do simple jobs quickly and more safely. In doing so they employ simple movements effectively.

These two very different machines show that what at first sight appear to be sophisticated and complex devices are in fact very similar and use basic movements: turning, sliding, swinging.

A mechanical digger

Simple Machines

Machines have become so important in our lives today that we have a machine to do almost every task. Because we have so many machines around us we often do not notice them or even realize that some of these devices are machines.

We give them a variety of labels and take what they do and how they do it for granted.

You may have heard of these words: gadget, thingumajig, tool, instrument, contraption, electronic device.

To understand machines we don't have to look at exotic or expensive devices. We all use a variety of machines every day. We may call these things many different names but they are really very simple machines.

They use the basic movements, either singularly or combined.

The sliding, swinging and turning movements are made by screw-threads, lever arms, wheels, pivots, etc.

Just take a look at some of the devices shown here.

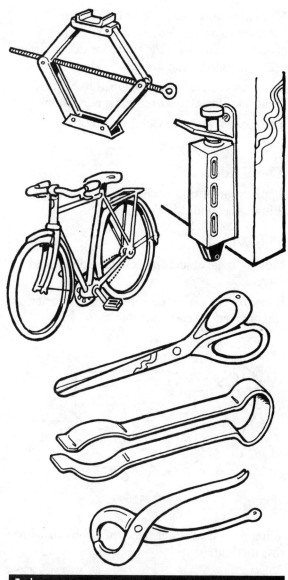

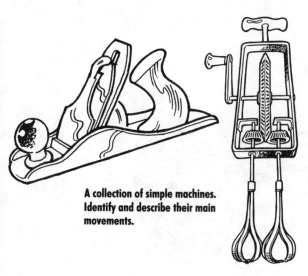

A collection of simple machines. Identify and describe their main movements.

Task

(a) Can you think of other simple machines?

(b) Can you tell which type of movements are being used?

(c) Now the hard bit – can it be further simplified or improved?

11

2 Helping Hand

An Early Start

Human beings are rarely satisfied with themselves or their environment. Earlier civilizations have set the trend for our desire to create labour-saving devices.

Many ways have been developed to help us create comfortable and suitable conditions.

The earliest known machines can be called *tools*.

The Wedge

Application of this can be seen in a variety of things. Can you think of some?

The Wheel

Moving large objects presented problems to solve.

Large blocks placed on rollers reduced friction and allowed for easy movement.

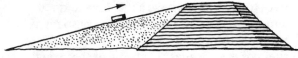

Using a sand wedge!

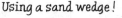

The pyramids under construction.

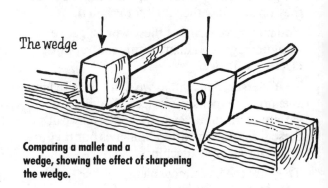

The wedge

Comparing a mallet and a wedge, showing the effect of sharpening the wedge.

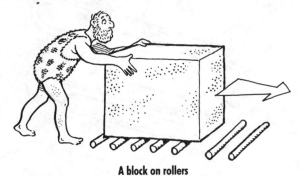

A block on rollers

What do you consider to be the problem with this method?

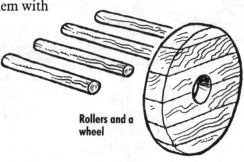

Rollers and a wheel

First Machines

The Lever

A large **lever** can easily move a heavy object.
The two can also be combined to perform
complex tasks, like water-lifting devices that
use a counterbalance.

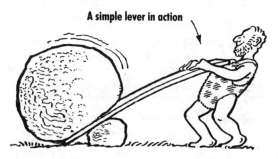

A simple lever in action

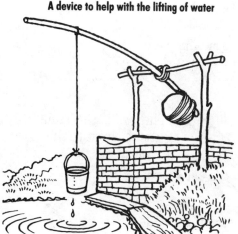

A device to help with the lifting of water

Some very interesting structures and devices
were designed by early civilizations. Many
monuments which they erected are large and
constructed of very heavy materials. We still
don't know how these stones were moved or
lifted. How do you think they managed to
construct the following?

- Stonehenge
- The Easter Island statues
- The Pyramids

Task

Take a closer look at everyday objects which
help us and which we use without thinking.
Try to identify the simple machines and
principles, such as the lever, wheel, screw-
thread, etc.

Here is a list of some of the objects. You may
think of others.

- scissors
- sugar tongs
- PrittSticks
- spanners
- hand vice
- tap

Can you explain how these objects use the
basic principles?

13

Helping Hand

Levers . . .

All levers have three things in common: the effort (where you do the pushing), the load (the thing that resists the pushing) and the pivot or fulcrum (the point round which the first two revolve).

An old-fashioned tin-opener is a good example of a simple lever.

Effort is here moving the opener up and down

The load is the blade cutting through the tin, which resists the effort.

The fulcrum is where the opener rests on the edge of the tin can.

An old-style tin-opener

Effort

Load

Fulcrum

A schematic drawing of the old tin-opener

Now let us examine a more modern tin-opener.

The wedge does the cutting and the can is turned by the butterfly.

This is another lever similar to the key. Can you spot the load, effort and fulcrum?

The load is the blade cutting the can.

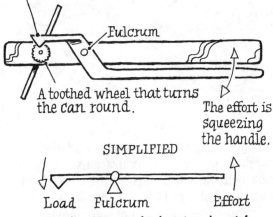

Fulcrum

A toothed wheel that turns the can round.

The effort is squeezing the handle.

SIMPLIFIED

Load   Fulcrum   Effort

A more modern tin-opener also shown in a schematic form.

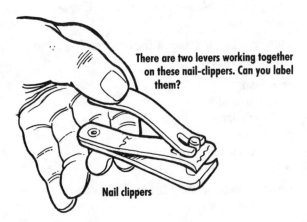

There are two levers working together on these nail-clippers. Can you label them?

Nail clippers

Task 1

Look around your home and find more examples of levers. Identify the load, effort and fulcrum in each case.

... and Linkages

By connecting levers together, we can make some useful objects.

Have you considered how the pedal bin works? It is an example of simple **linkage**. The act of pressing your foot down on the pedal works a lever which pushes up a rod at the back of the bin. This rod is connected to the lid, which is pivoted at the back, thus causing the lid to rise.

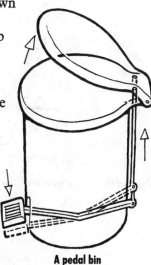

A pedal bin

Try to construct a model of the levers involved, using cardboard. The measurements need to be accurate to achieve the correct movement.

By changing the position of the load, effort and fulcrum, you find three different arrangements. These are called different classes of lever.

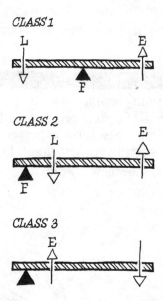

Task 2

Go back over all the levers described so far and identify them.

What class of lever is the key?

Helping Hand

Ups ...

Linkages are not easily understood and seem to have a magical quality. Could you describe how an umbrella works?

When the slider is moved up the shaft, the linkage forces the umbrella open.

What would happen if there was no material on the frame?

Task 1

Can you identify another linkage very similar to this which is found in people's gardens? This time its purpose is not to prevent you from getting wet but to help things to dry.

Draw it and show how it works.

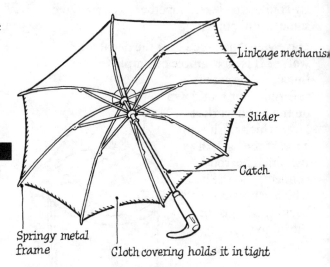

Linkage mechanism

Slider

Catch

Springy metal frame

Cloth covering holds it in tight

An umbrella opened up to show the linkages

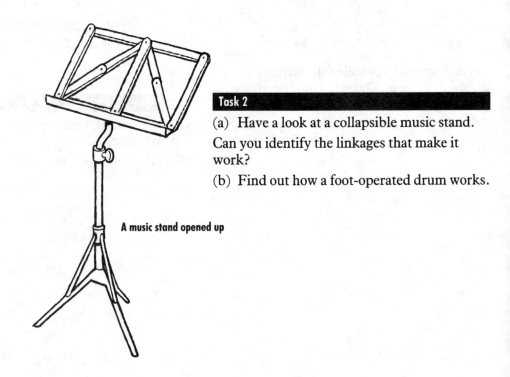

A music stand opened up

Task 2

(a) Have a look at a collapsible music stand. Can you identify the linkages that make it work?

(b) Find out how a foot-operated drum works.

... and Downs

Linkages can be used to help us extend our reach. For instance, when picking apples or for helping people who cannot bend easily to pick things up.

Another good example of where human hands cannot cope, and so extensions are built in to help, is on woodwind musical instruments.

On this flute our fingers cannot reach all the holes necessary to play the notes: the linkages act as extensions to the fingers.

A grabber/fruit picker

Squeeze here and the grip closes.

A flute showing the keys extended by linkages

Task 3

Look at other musical instruments? Can you work out how a piano works?

Linkages at work again.

You may have seen this type of device on cars. It is a simple linkage arrangement. Can you suggest why this device might be used?

What kind of material would it be made of?

Car window security device, with parallel linkages

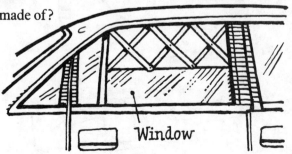

Window

Helping Hand

Moving On

The need to move large objects and the desire to make this task easier probably led to one of the most important inventions – the **wheel**. It is not too much of an exaggeration to say that if we did not have the wheel, many tasks would be impossible.

Just take a look at your own surroundings.

The first wheel was most likely to have been made out of a number of parts.

Different ancient cultures arrived at the idea of the wheel in many different ways and at different times – sometimes almost a thousand years apart!

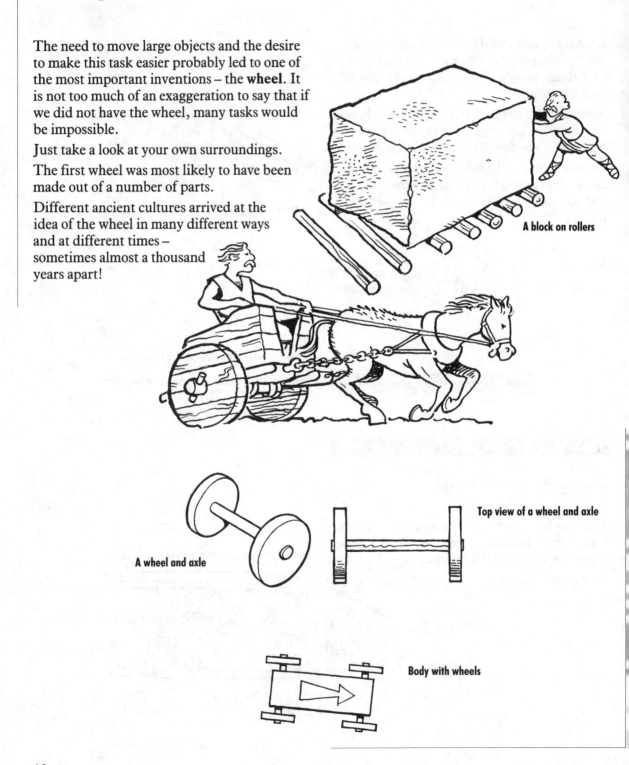

A block on rollers

A wheel and axle

Top view of a wheel and axle

Body with wheels

Moving Further On

What happens when you turn a corner?

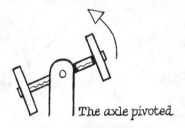

The axle pivoted.

The **axle** allows the wheel to turn over and over. This made it possible to use the wheel for such things as wagons, chariots, etc.

The wheel soon became a pulley and a gear.

Wheel and pulley

The Windlass

Here is a simple pulley system that has been in use for hundreds of years. Can you identify the parts that have made the lifting of the bucket easier? Can you construct a model to see how the supports might be added and how they would help or hinder movement?

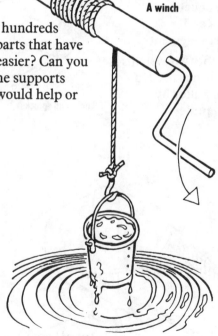

A winch

Pulleys ...

From a wheel, it is only a small jump to create a mechanical system of transferring energy from one point to another by connecting two wheels with a belt.

What would happen if we were to use this method of transferring motion from one pulley to another?

This system can be useful as it stands. With a slight modification to the wheels and the belt we can stop the belt from sliding off the wheel.

Can you design a new **pulley and belt** system so that the belt does not slip off?

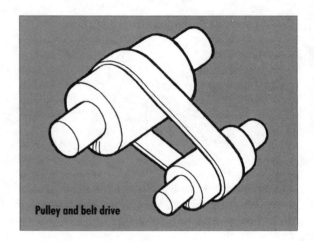

Pulley and belt drive

Chain and Sprocket

Some problems of a belt and pulley system have been overcome with a **sprocket and chain**. What are the advantages and disadvantages of this type of arrangement?

To complete the link between the two systems using new materials, a mechanism is needed for the accurate rotation of one pulley by another – the **toothed belt and pulley**.

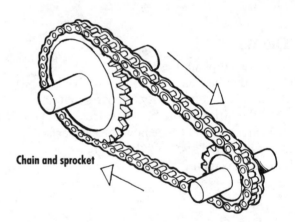

Chain and sprocket

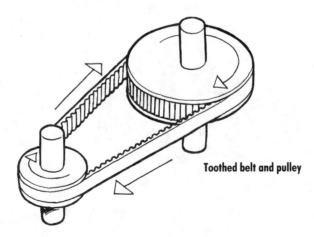

Toothed belt and pulley

... and Gears

Gears

Fixing pegs to a wheel transforms it into a gear. It is not known when the first gear was used and how. However, as we know what materials were used we can speculate as to what it may have looked like.

It is clear that a wooden gear-wheel constructed like this would have many problems, all of which would reduce its efficiency.

It was only a matter of time before gears were made to fit accurately into each other. We call this *meshing*.

Wooden gears meshing and a gear wheel.

A gear wheel

Task 1

Why do you think that the tooth of a gear-wheel is shaped as it is and not with a sharp point?

Types of Gears

Gears transfer rotary motion from one shaft to another without slipping. There are many types of gears because of the number of different type of movements that are required.

Task 2

Can you work out where these gears might be used and what each type is called?

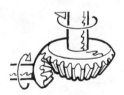

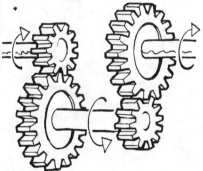

A collection of gears

Helping Hand

Round . . .

What do this vacuum cleaner, sash-window and washing-machine have in common? Answer: they all rely on *pulleys* to make them work.

A pulley is a wheel with a groove in the outside edge with a rope or belt passing over it.

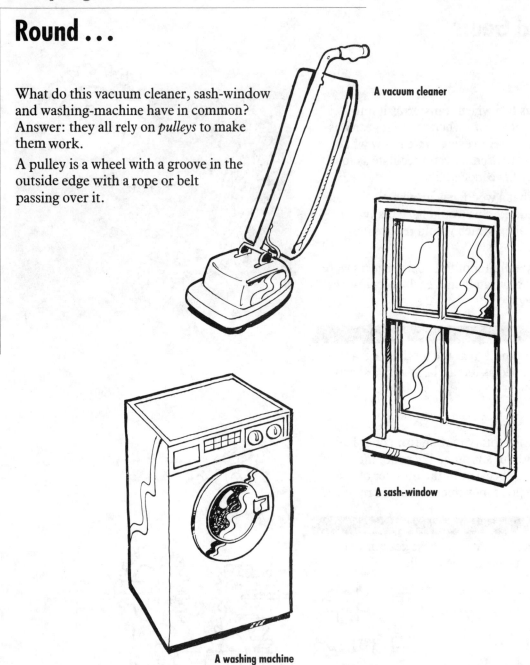

A vacuum cleaner

A sash-window

A washing machine

... and Round

In a sash-window a rope is attached to the window at one end and passes over a pulley fixed in the frame, to a weight attached to the other end. As the window is lifted up the weight is lowered, balancing the window.

The workings of a sash-window

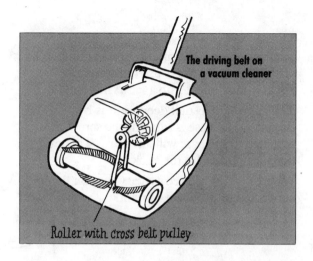

The driving belt on a vacuum cleaner

Roller with cross belt pulley

The pulley in the vacuum cleaner performs a different function.

The motor turns the spindle which drives the beater round by means of a belt drive.

This belt is twisted to change the direction and the axis of rotation.

What happens if the two pulleys are of different sizes?

The drum inside the washing-machine turns at varying speeds.

A pulley is driven by an electric motor. The belt links the motor to the drum.

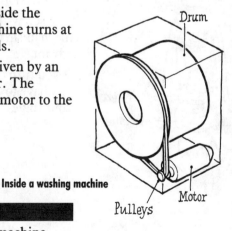

Inside a washing machine

Task

Why is the pulley on the washing-machine motor so small and the pulley on the drum so large?

Helping Hand

The Screw-Thread

The screw-thread gives us a great deal of accurate control and an increase in effort. The screw-thread is always used to convert a circular movement into a *linear* motion.

The control of a stick deodorant is by a screw-thread. If the base is rotated, the screw-thread attached to the base will also turn. This pulls down or pushes up the stick.

Where else do you see a rotary motion being converted into a linear motion?

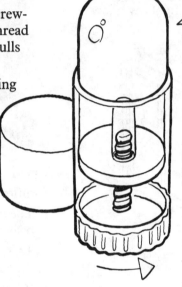

Picture of a deodorant with a cutaway showing the screw-thread.

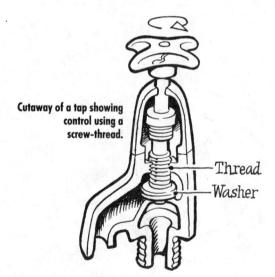

Cutaway of a tap showing control using a screw-thread.

Thread

Washer

The tap uses a screw-thread. Turning the tap on lifts the washer, which allows water to flow from the tap.

The screw-thread is an extensively used mechanism and gives us a large mechanical advantage.

If you turn on a tap fully, how much force do you have to use to stop the flow of water with your finger?

The Screw-Thread

Screw-thread as Control

If you place your thumbnail on a screw-thread and turn the thread you will notice that the thumbnail moves along the thread. The movement is very slow and hardly noticeable.

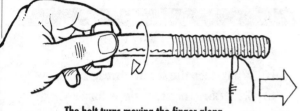

The bolt turns moving the finger along.

Here, the screw-thread is converting a rotary motion into a linear motion.

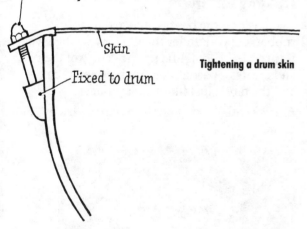

Nut turns, pulls down on bracket and stretches skin.

Skin

Tightening a drum skin

Fixed to drum

A good example of control using a screw-thread can be seen in the tightening of a drum-skin. One revolution of the nut tightens the skin by the pitch of the thread. A great degree of accuracy is needed to produce the correct note. The screw-thread gives this control.

Now substitute a small gear for the thumbnail. (See diagram.) In this new arrangement the rotary motion is converted to another rotary motion but we have changed the axis. Therefore we have converted both the direction and the position. This arrangement is used in another musical instrument, the guitar. Here a large number of turns of the key are required to turn the gear once – again providing a great deal of control.

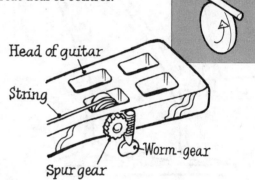

Head of guitar

String

Worm-gear

Spur gear

We call this mechanism a **worm-gear** and worm-wheel.

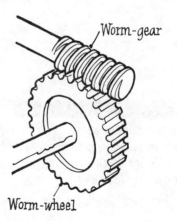

Worm-gear

Worm-wheel

Helping Hand

Hold On

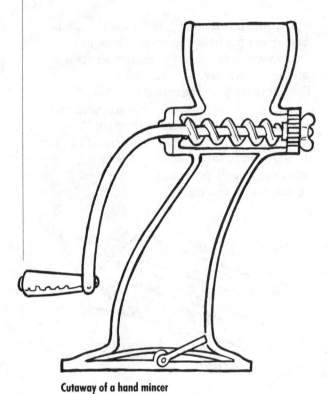

Cutaway of a hand mincer

The diagram shows a cutaway view of a mincer.

Study the drawing carefully and look at the key features such as the handle, the shape of the stem, and the screw-thread.

Task 1

(a) Can you explain why the handle is so long?

(b) What does the screw-thread do?

(c) Why does the stem slope forward?

These are interesting mechanisms, but there is one more which is not so obvious. If you have used a mincer to mince up meat you will know that it is quite hard work. Hence the long handle, which must also be held down firmly.

Holding Firmly

The lever on the base is attached to a rubberized pad under the mincer. As the lever is turned, the loop lifts up the centre of the pad and creates a partial vacuum between the pad and the table, just like a sink plunger.

A lever with a loop like this is also called a **cam**.

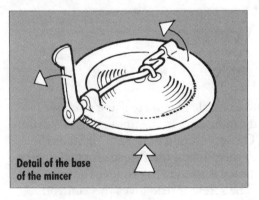

Detail of the base of the mincer

Task 2

Look at the mincer again. The suction pad system is not always practical. Why? Can you design another method of holding down the mincer on a table-top?

Clues: G-cramp, machine vice, clip-on lamps.

Hold On

Holding on with a Cam

Cleats on a sailing boat allow a very quick way of adjusting and holding a rope.

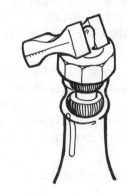

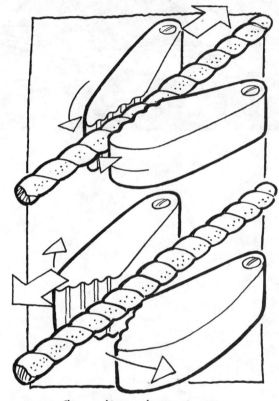

Cleats working on a boat to grip a rope

When the rope is pulled in one direction the cleat will open, allowing the rope to travel through. When the rope is pulled in the opposite direction the cleat will close and grip the rope. Normally the cleats are sprung shut.

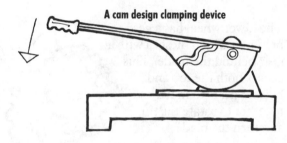

A cam design clamping device

There are other ways of using a cam as a clamping device. The diagram above shows a drilling clamp. The long handle with a cam presses the material down on to a drilling machine, holding it firmly flat.

You will have noticed that a cam performs an important function. It changes a turning (*rotary*) motion into a straight up-and-down (*linear*) motion.

Task 3

Study the three examples and with the aid of sketches explain the actions of the three types of cams.

Making the Going Easier ...

We have looked at two tin-openers already but, even with the lever that operates the wedge and the butterfly handles to help turn the can around, there are still many people who are unable to use it.

Here is another system which has been designed to overcome some of these problems. In this method the wedge has been swapped for a rotary blade, and two cogs are also added to grip and rotate the can when the handle is turned.

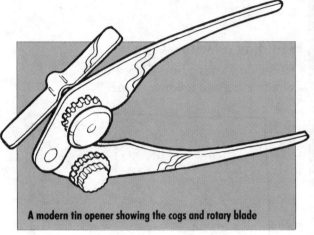

A modern tin opener showing the cogs and rotary blade

The butterfly handle acts as a lever.

The single action of the butterfly handle turns one gear and the rotary blade.

The lower wheel has a gear behind it which meshes with a gear behind the blade. This causes both the top and bottom gears to move together to rotate the tin and turn the blade.

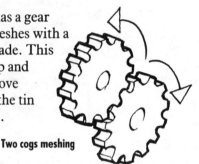

Two cogs meshing

Task 1

Is it possible to improve this design further?
Clues: motor, magnet.

... and Easier

Where else can we find gears?

Have you ever made a meringue? If you have, you know that beating the egg whites is hard work with a hand whisk.

Mixing bowl and whisk

Using a hand whisk which has gears makes the going a lot easier.

Can you see how many more teeth there are on the large gear? Why don't we use the same size gears?

If you turn the handle once, can you guess how many turns the whisk will make?

In the diagram shown, could both whisks turn in the same direction?

A detail showing the bevel gears

Hand whisk, showing bevel gears

Task 2

(a) Is it possible to use a motor to turn the whisk?

(b) How would the motor be connected?

(c) Would we use this arrangement of gears when we use a motor?

29

3 Movement

Floor ...

Schematic diagram of a lift

As buildings are being built higher and higher there has to be a quick and easy way to travel between floors. Running up stairs to the twentieth floor is no fun.

The lift provides the opportunity to design and build tall office blocks.

The lift is raised or lowered by a cable passing over a large pulley which is connected to a motor. The simplified diagram (*left*) shows how this can be achieved. The **counterbalance** is very useful.

Task 1

(a) Can you suggest why a counterbalance is useful?

(b) How does the lift know when it is exactly at a floor level?

(c) List some safety measures you would take when designing a lift system.

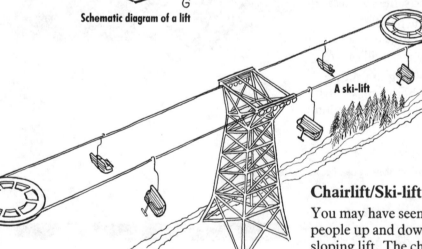

A ski-lift

Chairlift/Ski-lift

You may have seen a chairlift which carries people up and down a mountain. It is like a sloping lift. The chairs are fixed to the cable, which is pulled round by the large pulleys at the top and bottom.

Task 2

Where is the counterbalance in a chairlift?

... to Floor

Another way to move from floor to floor is by using the escalator. This also uses a pulley system to lift people up and down.

We have considered three ways of moving people from floor to floor. Can you work out which mechanical systems are most likely to be used for each of the lifts?

A simplified diagram of an escalator

A Simple Lift System

This is usually called a winch. Here, the bucket is used to raise water from a well. Using the sizes given can you calculate:

  (a) How far the bucket rises with one turn of the handle?

  (b) How far the handle moves in one turn?

  (c) What do you think would happen if the length of the handle was reduced?

  (d) What would happen if you increased the size of the drum?

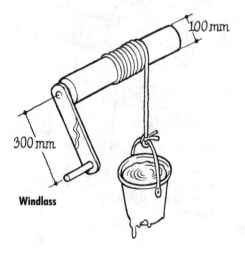

100 mm

300 mm

Windlass

Movement

Taking a Closer Look

The bicycle uses many of the mechanisms that we have looked at so far. Can you identify the key features? Look for levers, linkages, gears, wheels, axle, cranks, pulleys, etc.

To do this successfully you have to isolate parts of the bike and look at each from a different angle. For example, the handlebar is a lever. Can you work out where the fulcrum, load and effort are on the handlebar and steering mechanism?

Where might you see a **crank**?

What sort of arrangements are used to drive the rear wheel?

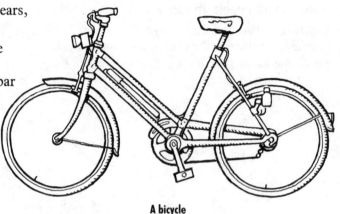

A bicycle

The **dynamo** is shown on the rear wheel. Can you find out what the dynamo does? Can you explain how it works?

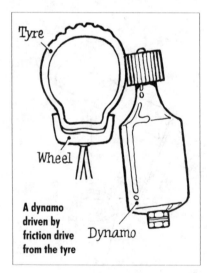

Tyre

Wheel

A dynamo driven by friction drive from the tyre

Dynamo

Task 1

If the dynamo head has a diameter of 20 mm and the bicycle wheel has a diameter of 650 mm, how many times does the dynamo rotate with one turn of the wheel?

Taking a Closer Look

Task 2

If the crank wheel has 36 teeth and is turned once, the chain will move a distance of 36 teeth. As it moves it will pull the gears round by 36 teeth.

The first gear will make one full turn for the first 24 teeth and a half turn for the remaining 12 teeth. So the rear wheel will turn one-and-a-half times for one turn of the crank when it is in first gear.

Can you work out the number of times the rear wheel will turn in the other four gears?

What difference will it make to the bike's performance if the rear wheel is either larger or smaller?

Gear Ratio

Number of teeth on driver: number of teeth on driven = Gear ratio

$$36:24 \qquad = 1.5:1$$

Can you work out the gear ratio for the other gears?

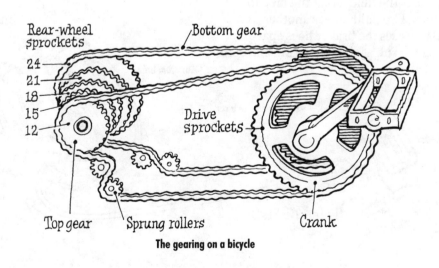

The gearing on a bicycle

33

Movement

Stop . . .

Brakes are always necessary when you are operating a moving object. Many types of brakes use levers to push something on to the moving part to slow it down.

Squeezing the brake lever pulls the cable which is connected to a brake mechanism. As the cable is pulled the levers are moved upwards and inwards, thus pressing the brake-blocks against the rim of the wheel. Here we see an example of friction being very useful.

Can you explain why we use rubber blocks for the brakes? Is there anything else which could be used?

The cable is a very useful method of transferring motion. Levers and linkages were once used to operate bicycle brakes. How do you think they worked?

Why don't we use them any more?

In a car, a similar method is used to stop. Instead of a cable, a fluid contained within a tube is used to transfer the motion. When the brake pedal of a car is compressed, this cylinder pushes the fluid along the pipe to the brake system. The fluid moves another cylinder that forces the brake shoes apart, causing them to rub against the drum and stop the wheel.

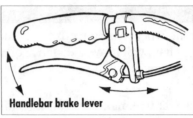

Handlebar brake lever

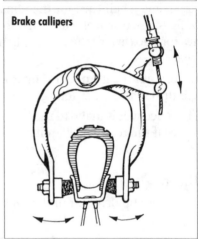

Brake callipers

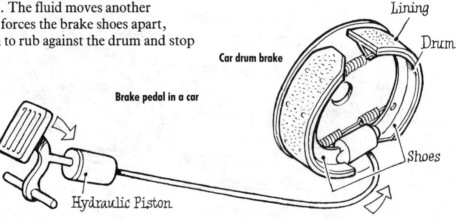

Car drum brake

Lining

Drum

Shoes

Brake pedal in a car

Hydraulic Piston

... and Go

There are many different types of brakes and braking systems which use levers, oil and air. Investigate different types of braking systems and explain why a particular method is chosen for the purpose.

We don't always want to stop the whole machine. In a bicycle you can stop pedalling and still keep moving. A car may be stationary but the engine can still be running. A special device is needed for this purpose. We call this device a **clutch**. Unlike other mechanisms, clutches tend to be hidden. However, if you carefully study the diagrams on this page, it should become clear how the device works.

In a car, we don't want to stop the engine running whenever we have to stop. So, we 'cut off' the engine (connected to the driver shaft) from the wheels (connected to the driven shaft).

DISENGAGED

Driver shaft rotating   Driven shaft stationary

ENGAGED

Schematic diagram of a car's clutch

Car clutches are very much more complex than this, but the principle is the same.

Inside the rear wheel of a bicycle there is a mechanism called a pawl and ratchet. The pawl is sprung and will push against the ratchet. If the ratchet is turned clockwise, the pawl will engage in one of the teeth and will be turned, so turning the central axle. If the ratchet is turned anti-clockwise, the pawl will slip round, making the familiar clicking noise, and the axle will be disengaged.

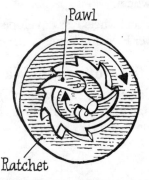

Pawl

Ratchet

Pawl and ratchet working as a clutch

Friction is not all bad: for example, in clutches and brakes we use it to our advantage, i.e., to stop and go.

Wind and Water

Water-wheels

We have been using water as a source of energy to produce useful movement for centuries. Some of these machines are still in use today.

Over the years the designs of water-wheels have changed and improved.

The earliest water-wheels were designed as shown. Water was directed by a chute on to a horizontal wheel.

Later, a vertical wheel was developed to gain greater power by using bigger wheels.

Changing the Motion with Water

Water flowing along a race (channel) or directed to fall on to a water-wheel changes a linear motion to a rotary motion.

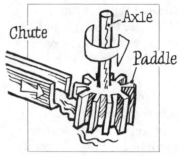

Horizontal and vertical water-wheels

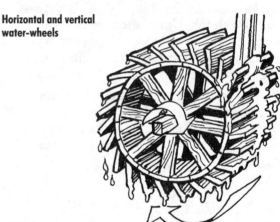

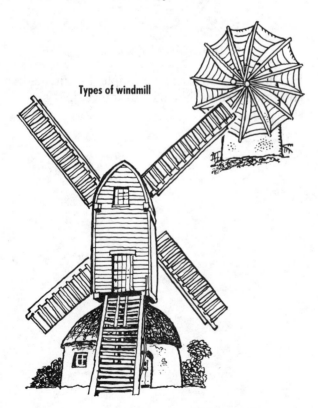

Types of windmill

Windmills

Wind is also a useful source of energy. Just as the water-wheel uses water to produce movement, windmills harness the force of wind by using similar paddles, only fewer. These are called sails.

Many types of windmills have been built over the years. The rotary motion produced by water-wheels and windmills was mainly used for grinding grain, or pumping water out of mines.

Now a new breed of windmills has been developed to generate electricity from the wind.

Wind and Water

You will find all of these types of gears in many water-wheels and windmills. They are shown as being driven by the axle. As you can see, the gears all do different things. Thus almost any type of movement can be created.

Different types of gears

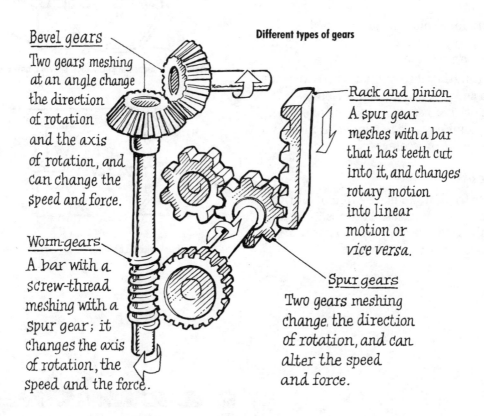

Bevel gears
Two gears meshing at an angle change the direction of rotation and the axis of rotation, and can change the speed and force.

Worm-gears
A bar with a screw-thread meshing with a spur gear; it changes the axis of rotation, the speed and the force.

Rack and pinion
A spur gear meshes with a bar that has teeth cut into it, and changes rotary motion into linear motion or vice versa.

Spur gears
Two gears meshing change the direction of rotation, and can alter the speed and force.

Free-wheeling

When there is movement between parts of machines there is a need to consider two other factors: *lubrication* and *bearings*. Both of these enable smooth running of moving parts.

Lubrication

Where machine components are attached or located together and are in moving contact, we are faced with **friction**.

Friction can be useful, but not where we want a smooth and efficient motion. Friction prevents two surfaces from moving over each other. It is not possible to remove friction, but its effect can be overcome with lubricants.

Lubricants

To reduce friction, we place a film of lubricant between the two surfaces. The most commonly-used lubricant is oil. There are other types, e.g., grease or water.

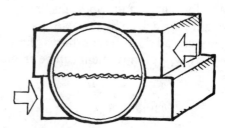

Two surfaces seen under the microscope showing how rough they are.

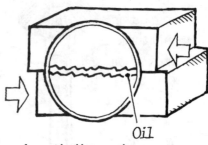

The same surfaces with oil between them

Task 1

Where food is prepared by machinery, water is used to lubricate machine parts.

   (a) Why do you think this is?

   (b) What sort of materials do you think the machinery would be made from where food is prepared?

Lubrication

Methods of Lubricating

Many different methods have been devised in order to get the oil or grease to where it matters.

In most cases the oil is applied by hand and using special cans. Sometimes the lubricant is placed in a reservoir from where it travels to the point of contact.

When oil needs to be applied to hidden parts, other methods are used, such as the splash method. A gearbox is filled with oil. The oil is picked up by the lowest gear and passed around through meshing gears.

Oiling a bearing

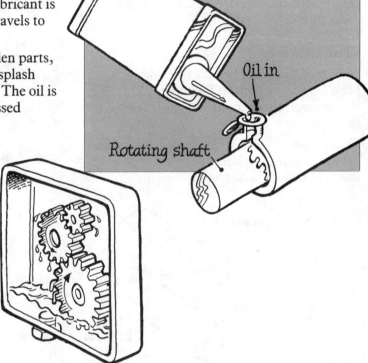

Oil in

Rotating shaft

The splash method of lubricating

Task 2

Oil comes in a variety of grades. You may have seen a tin of oil with the codes 20/50 W or SAE 20 W. These codes refer to the thickness of the oil and the changes it can cope with in fluctuating temperatures.

Try and find out where these codes came from and why they are necessary

Rolling On

Bearings

Bearings also allow for smooth running, but they have another important role: to support a moving part.

The moving part may need support in any direction because the forces acting upon it may come from separate directions.

Plain Bearings

The simplest type of bearing is known as a *plain bearing*, or bush. It is really a well-fitting sleeve which allows a rotating bar to turn with ease.

These types of bearings are made from either bronze or plastic. Where noise reduction is essential the plastic bearing is chosen.

The shoulder stops the shaft from sliding through the bearing.

A shouldered shaft

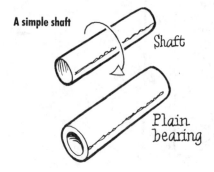

A simple shaft

Shaft

Plain bearing

Task 1

Can you speculate where you might see plastic bearings? Try to think of household items.

Bearings

Ball-bearings

The main reason for using bearings is to create a more efficient machine. This can be achieved if friction is reduced.

Since friction is caused by two parts rubbing against one another, all that needs to happen is to allow the minimum of contact between two materials. Ball-bearings do this very well.

The diagram shows ball-bearings and their contact points. It is clear that friction is reduced substantially.

Roller Bearings

When there is a need to support a long, heavy turning bar then a slight change is needed. Here we use the same principles of reducing the surface contact by using *rollers*.

Both the rollers and balls are in sleeves so that the bearing is manageable.

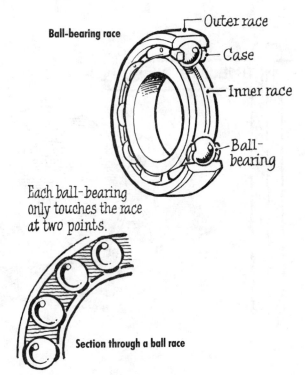

Ball-bearing race

Outer race
Case
Inner race
Ball-bearing

Each ball-bearing only touches the race at two points.

Section through a ball race

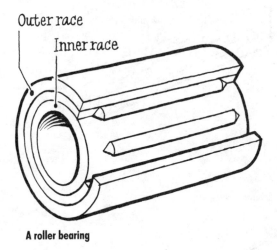

Outer race
Inner race

A roller bearing

Task 2

Non-stop Machines

(a) Is it possible to have a machine that never stops?

(b) Is there such a thing as a perpetual motion?

(c) Try to find out about some of the machines that have been designed to perpetuate motion.

Clues: Leonardo da Vinci, Archimedes.

4 Measurement

Scale ...

Getting things right is very important. Making things work requires accurate measurement.

So this sign to Timbuktu is nonsense and playing football on a miniature pitch with a large ball would be difficult.

In order to make things work for us, accurate and appropriate methods of measurement are needed. There are many different ways of measuring, as many as there are things to measure:

distance, weight, pressure, volume, length, temperature, level, speed.

When measuring some things we measure a change, for example, in temperature, weight and speed. How do you think we could measure change accurately?

What does a spirit level measure?

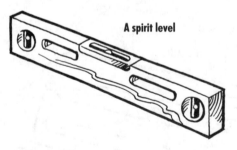

A spirit level

Task 1

Callipers are used for many different types of measurement. They are available in different sizes and for external or internal uses. How is the measurement read? Do you think this is an accurate method?

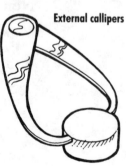

External callipers

42

... and Size

Measuring Weight

Weighing machines can come in many different forms. You may have seen a device like this before. It employs a linkage.

Why do you think the pointer is on the longest lever of the linkage?

The linkage is known as parallel linkage. Why do you think this is used? What function does the spring perform in this device?

Weighing scales using a parallel linkage

Measuring Distance

An odometer measures lengths of roads. The wheel is pushed along the road and the measurement is read on a meter fixed at an angle for convenience.

Can you suggest a way this device would work?

The odometer

Accurate Measurement

Accurate measurement requires amplification of the change. To measure a small change accurately, the scale must allow fine adjustment and enlargement of the movement. A micrometer does this very well. It uses a screw-thread.

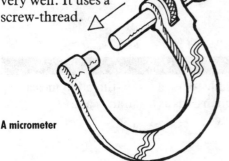

A micrometer

Task 2

(a) Find out about the micrometer and explain, using the words *pitch, lead, scale, amplification*. How does the device measure so accurately?

(b) How are ball-bearings measured?

Measurement

How Long?

When we need to measure anything, the first task is to work out the type of measurement needed. The scale of measurement also gives clues to the device we can use.

Small Measurements

If the item to be measured is small, a rule will suffice. If the object to be measured has a flat surface the task is easy, but a spherical item can present problems. Using callipers can help, but they need to be read using a rule.

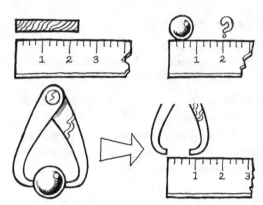

Measuring with callipers

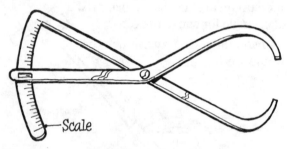

New callipers with a scale.

Is it possible to make callipers with extended levers and also to incorporate a scale which would give a more accurate reading?

How would you begin to make the scale so that an accurate measurement can be read?

Very Accurate Measurement

The micrometer (page 43) is very much more accurate than the old callipers, or even our new and refined callipers.

Long Distance

The tape-measure can measure up to 3, 5 and 100 metres. It all depends on the length of the tape and the purpose. The tape-measure is made from a flexible material. It is made convenient to use by being coiled-up, spring-loaded and having a cam lock. What do you think these additions do?

What about measuring awkward distances single-handed? Can we use a screw-thread?

Task 1

Is it possible to use a screw-thread to measure larger dimensions as accurately as a micrometer?

How Far?

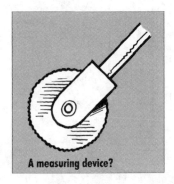

A measuring device?

This device allows us to measure a room and curved surfaces. Can you explain how the device works? How do we draw up the scale? Is it more accurate than a rule?

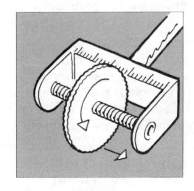

In order to measure very long distances, for example, roads or public paths, a much larger and more durable device has to be considered. A crude version can be made up using a *facecut gear* on a wheel with a small pinion meshing and driving a worm-gear. This kind of device could present problems. Can you suggest what they might be?

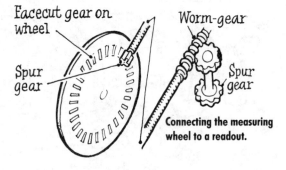

Facecut gear on wheel

Spur gear

Worm-gear

Spur gear

Connecting the measuring wheel to a readout.

For measuring roads and other long distances we use a device called an odometer. The device is very similar to the one described above but the movement is transferred using sealed systems of gears and cables. Do you know which types of gears would be used to indicate distances travelled?

Clue: reduction in rotation.

The odometer

Counting

There are many measurements which are made possible by having a simple machine that can count for us.

Here is an example of an ancient counting machine.

This device was used to count the number of times that an ox had walked round while turning a grindstone. The disc was attached to the stone shaft. With every turn, a ball would drop through the hole and into the box. A man could count the balls and so know the number of turns made.

By connecting the drive of the stone to the counting device by a worm and worm-wheel, instead of counting in ones they could count in tens, or twelves. Can you explain this in more detail?

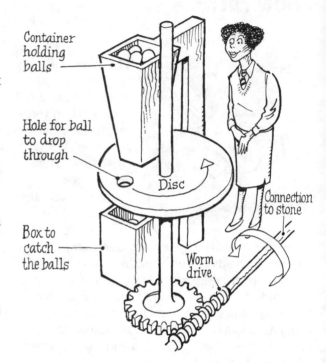

A counting device familiar to all of us is the speedometer in a car. It will indicate the speed of travel and it will also record how far we have travelled. The diagram below shows how gears are used to give a counter in units, tens, hundreds, thousands, etc. of miles or kilometres.

The tenths of a mile drum is driven by a drive from the gearbox. This drum rotates in a calculated way: exactly one complete rotation for every mile travelled. The problem is then to make the next drum move round one step at a time.

The right-hand side of each drum has two projecting teeth for each number. A small gear-wheel fits into these teeth and pushes the drums round one step at a time. The small gear holds the secret of how it only moves one step at a time. The small gear has alternate wide and narrow teeth. The left-hand side of each drum has only two teeth placed together

The mile counter in a car

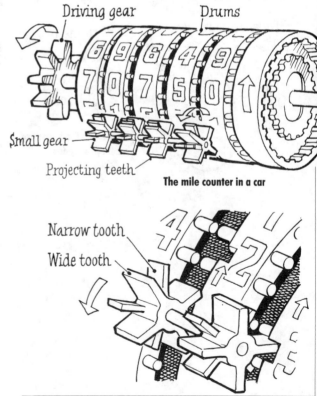

Counting

with a slot between. As the teeth and slot make contact with the small gear once every revolution, they turn it one place on, so moving the next drum up one number.

More modern technology works on digital electronics. Simple pulses of electrical current trip an electrical switch that is registered on a digital readout.

Counting objects is all very well, but if we can measure how long something has taken, we can then indicate speed.

The speed of a moving object is the distance divided by the time taken. So we have miles *per* hour.

The diagram below shows just how land speed records are measured.

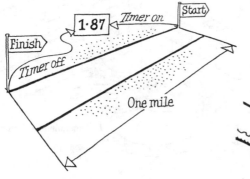

It is of course impossible to measure the speed of a car going down the high street this way, so we need an instrument that will indicate accurately to the driver how fast a car is travelling.

On a bicycle, the front wheel has a peg attached to it that moves the mileometer round. This system is too crude for a car, so the speedo drive is connected to the main drive coming out of the gearbox. The actual connection is by a worm-gear. Can you say why?

Inside the speedo the drive spins a magnet round its centre. Just above this magnet there is a disc of metal that is held steady by a hair-spring. The disc has magnetic properties and so will try to move as the magnet moves. As the magnet spins, the disc also tries to spin, but it is held back by the spring. As the magnet spins faster the disc tries even harder to follow and the spring gives a little.

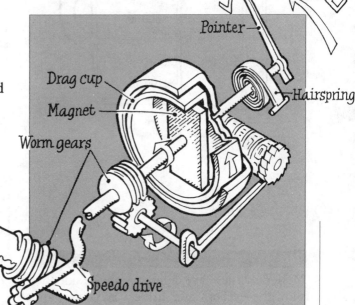

The workings of a speedometer

The disc is now reacting to how fast the magnet spins, so by using a pointer attached to the disc we can calibrate the speed of the car.

Consider the strength of the magnet and the spring.

Measurement

Full . . .

We all measure the volume of liquids for cooking, drinking and filling up the fuel tank of a car. Most of these activities are made straightforward by using a simple measuring jug. The smaller the diameter of the jug the more accurate we can be.

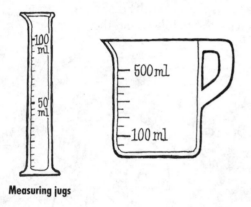

Measuring jugs

In building work it is sometimes necessary to know if two points, some distance apart, are at exactly the same height. Can you think where this should be necessary and why?

To do this there is a simple device using liquid in a clear tube. Water, or any liquid, will always find its own level. In the diagram of the kettle, the water in the kettle must be at the same level as the water in the measuring channel. So, with a long tube full of water, hold one end up against a wall, then move the other end up and down. When the water settles, the level of the water will be exactly the same at both ends.

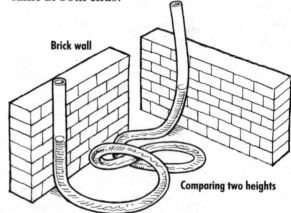

Brick wall

Comparing two heights

Task 1

Modern kettles have indicators on the side to show the level of water inside. Can you see any problems with this?

How much water is in the kettle?

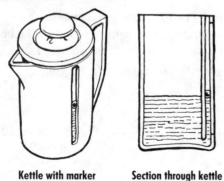

Kettle with marker   **Section through kettle**

... or Empty

Simple measuring jugs are no use when we cannot see the liquid that we want to measure, for example, in the fuel tank of a car. For these situations we need an automatic measuring system.

The lever comes to our aid again. In the tank a lever is suspended with a float attached to one end and an electrical contact to the other. The float will rise and fall according to the level of fuel in the tank and thus activate the lever. What class of lever is this? The pivot is in the middle, so, as the fuel drops, the contact will move round a variable resistance coil. Inside

the car a meter will show what the resistance of the coil is, so we can calibrate this reading in gallons or litres.

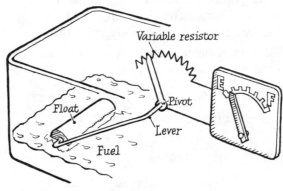

Fuel tank gauge

We cannot rely on our petrol gauge being sufficiently accurate for the garage attendant to be able to charge us the correct amount for the petrol that we buy. We therefore need a different method of measuring fuel.

We now need to examine how much liquid is passing a certain point along a pipe.

Here we can see a water-wheel in action. In this situation it is called an impeller. As the water flows through, the impeller will spin according to the volume of water. The drive from the impeller is connected through a worm and a gear train to a meter that will indicate the amount of water passing through.

This is very similar to the mileometer, already described, in counting the number of revolutions which an object makes.

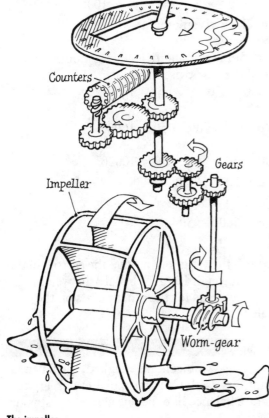

The impeller

Task 2

Can you think of further uses for these types of counting mechanisms?

Weighing It Up

It has always been important to know the weight of goods bought and sold. The need to know this measurement has ensured fantastic developments in weighing machines. There are now microelectronic machines which measure extremely accurately every time.

When we measure weight we actually measure a change. See if you can identify the change of state.

Beam Balance

The earliest forms of weighing used a simple lever in a state of equilibrium.

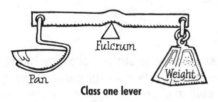

Class one lever

Here is a simple balance still used by traders in Asia to weigh groceries.

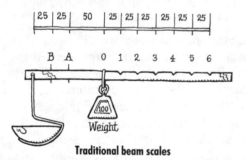

Traditional beam scales

The small weight is moved along the beam in steps. The steps are equally spaced and the weight is constant. The weight tends to move the balance in a clockwise (downwards) direction. The total of this force (the weight × distance from pivot) is called the clockwise moment. On the left-hand side of the beam is a pan which is also of a known weight. The beam can be held in equilibrium by holding a string at point A when the weight is at point 0.

The pan and contents will then provide the anticlockwise turning force, called the anticlockwise moment (weight of pan and contents × distance to pivot).

The moments turning the scales anticlockwise and clockwise are equal.

If we put some carrots into the pan and the weight has to move to point 2 to bring the balance into equilibrium, we can calculate the weight of the carrots (Wc).

weight of pan $100\,g = Wp$
known weight $100\,g = W$

Clockwise moment:
$W \times (50 + 25 + 25) = W \times 100$

Anticlockwise moment:
$(Wp + Wc) \times 50$
For equilibrium, anticlockwise moment must equal the clockwise moment.
So $(Wp + Wc) \times 50 = (100) \times W$

$Wp \times 50 + Wc \times 50 = 10000$

$100 \times 50 + Wc \times 50 = 10000$
$Wc \times 50 = 10000 - 5000$
$Wc \times 50 = 5000$
$Wc = 5000 \div 50$
$Wc = 100\,g$

So with the weight at point 2 the carrots in the pan will weigh $100\,g$. What are the weight measurements for the other points on the scale?

Task 1

When heavy objects are weighed, the balance point B is used. Can you explain this? Try to make a balance like the one above to test your theories.

Weighing It Up

Measuring the weight of a variety of things and/or people using a convenient method soon developed beyond a beam balance. The ability to measure without using complex balances or having a working knowledge of simple machines led to the development of spring-loaded balances.

A simple form of a spring balance.

The measurement on a spring balance is read from the extension of the spring. The extension of this spring is always constant, unless it is stretched beyond its limits. The scales would clearly state the maximum weight it could measure.

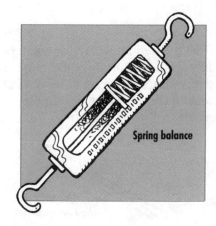

Spring balance

A Kitchen Scale

The spring is also used here, but this time a compression spring is employed. The compression is always constant with the load placed upon it. The advantage of this method is the convenient scale. A slight vertical movement is converted by a rack and pinion to a circular motion. The smaller the pinion, the greater the accuracy.

Weight

Rack and pinion

The workings of a set of kitchen scales

Bathroom Scales

Again, a rack and pinion is used but this time a tension spring is added to convert slight vertical movement to a large rotary movement.

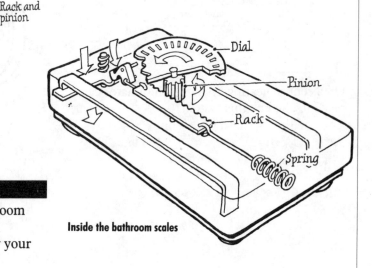

Dial

Pinion

Rack

Spring

Inside the bathroom scales

Task 2

Why do you think the dial on the bathroom scales spins past the pointer to a higher number before settling down to display your genuine weight?

Heat, Pressure . . .

Heat

Apart from the well-known thermometers which rely on the expansion of mercury to gauge temperature, there are other devices to measure temperature which use simple mechanisms.

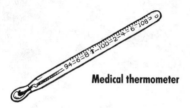

Medical thermometer

Heat detectors work on a **bimetallic strip** which is made up of two different metals.

As the strip heats it will bend downwards and as it cools it will bend upwards.

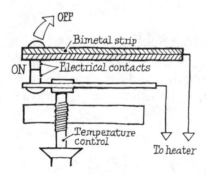

On a central heating system each radiator can be controlled by this system.

Pressure

Pressure can also be measured by using mercury. As you can imagine, there would be problems transporting the apparatus in an aeroplane in order to record its height above the ground.

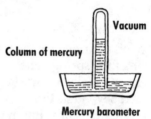

Mercury barometer

So to help pilots tell how high they are, a special **barometer** is used. Air pressure reduces as you climb higher, so an accurate height gauge can be made that actually measures air pressure: the aneroid barometer. In order to record the pressure, several levers and linkages magnify a small movement to give an accurate reading.

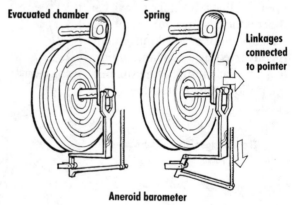

Aneroid barometer

... and Time

Time

Before digital microelectronic systems were developed, the accurate measurement of time was only possible with very fine mechanical clocks. These clocks were powered by a spring, which presented problems because the spring did not provide a uniform pulling force as it unwound.

The spring power is transmitted through a complex gear train to a small escape mechanism. As the balance wheel oscillates backwards and forwards, the escapement mechanism allows the escape wheel to turn one tooth at a time. This movement is transferred through the gears to allow the minute and hour hands to turn. The speed of oscillation of the balance wheel gives the accuracy of the clock itself.

With a pendulum clock you can vary its speed by changing either the length of the pendulum or the weight (or bob) at the end of it.

Task 1

Make a simple pendulum and test what happens if it is made longer or shorter. Then see what happens if you increase the weight of the bob.

Task 2

If the escape wheel has 12 teeth and it moves round at one tooth per second, can you work out how much reduction needs to be made to make the minute hand turn once per hour?

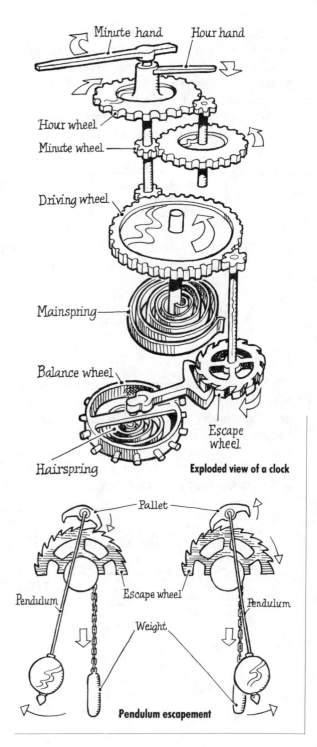

Exploded view of a clock

Pendulum escapement

5 Control

Control Systems

Controlling machines, the environment or the movement of people is vital if we are to benefit from technology. It is also true to say that, in general, control systems have developed after the machine/object has been designed. For example, we utilize control systems on a bicycle, washing-machine and heating systems.

The first bicycles did not have either a braking system or a clutch. The only way to stop the bicycle was to slowly rest your feet on the ground or fall off. The modern bicycle now has a free-wheeling hub and a sophisticated braking and gear system.

If we analyse this we find that control systems can be broken down into three basic parts.

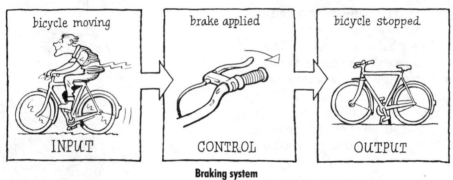

Braking system

Heating System

With an open coal fire, temperature control is very difficult. All you can do is add extra fuel or remove layers of clothes. Modern central heating systems have an automatic control system. This control system senses when the temperature has fallen below the desired level and switches the boiler on. When the desired temperature is reached it switches the boiler off.

We call this system a closed loop system. Other places where this is used are in modern washing-machines, anti-lock braking devices for cars, and pedestrian crossings.

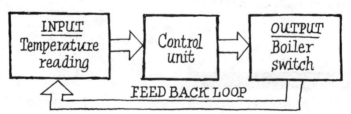

Control Systems

Traffic Lights as Control Systems

Traffic lights can be operated on an open or closed loop system. Where lights are working on a timeswitch and operating without knowledge of the cars on the road, an open loop is employed. At a pedestrian crossing a closed loop is used and the feedback is operated by the person crossing the road.

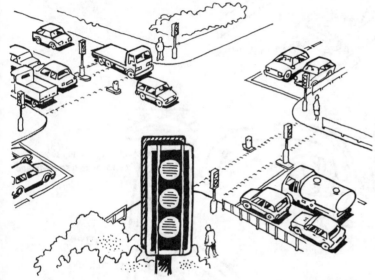

Some other more sophisticated systems use a way of counting the cars on a particular road and their approach to the junction. This is done by a vehicle detector buried beneath the road surface. The information is processed by a computer system which controls the lights.

As you can see, control systems do tend to involve more than mechanisms and often rely on electronics, pneumatics and/or microelectronics to work efficiently. However, it is possible to use simple control systems employing mechanical principles.

Think about how we can control water and its flow.

Task

Think of other places where we use control systems and plan out the block diagrams. Remember to label the *input–control–output–feedback*.

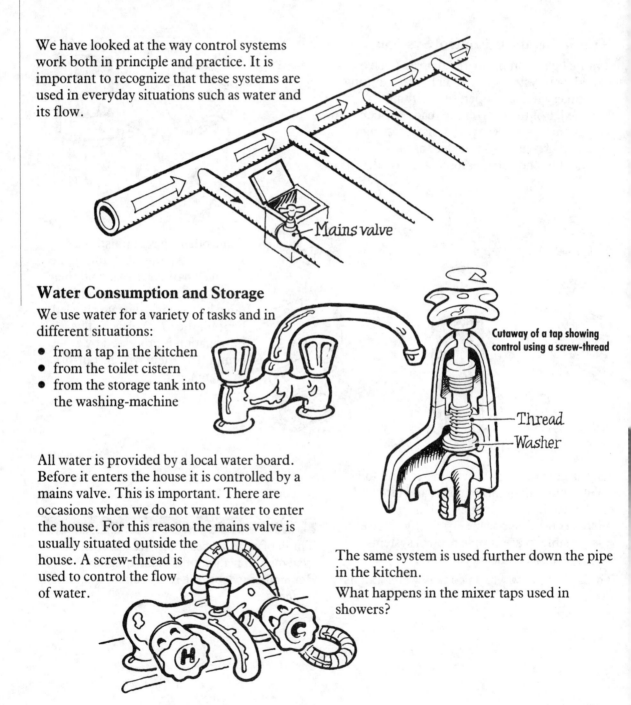

Control

Controlling Water

We have looked at the way control systems work both in principle and practice. It is important to recognize that these systems are used in everyday situations such as water and its flow.

Mains valve

Water Consumption and Storage

We use water for a variety of tasks and in different situations:

- from a tap in the kitchen
- from the toilet cistern
- from the storage tank into the washing-machine

Cutaway of a tap showing control using a screw-thread

Thread

Washer

All water is provided by a local water board. Before it enters the house it is controlled by a mains valve. This is important. There are occasions when we do not want water to enter the house. For this reason the mains valve is usually situated outside the house. A screw-thread is used to control the flow of water.

The same system is used further down the pipe in the kitchen.

What happens in the mixer taps used in showers?

Controlling Water

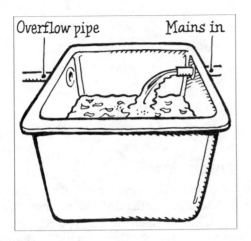

Overflow pipe   Mains in

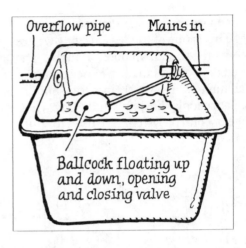

Overflow pipe   Mains in

Ballcock floating up and down, opening and closing valve

Storage Tank

Water is also piped to a storage tank (only in houses). This tank is usually kept full and thus it supplies all other uses around the home.

Since the mains supply is constantly entering the house we use other types of control devices to ensure that it does not flood the tank. Here we use two methods to prevent flooding indoors.

Ballcock

A ballcock allows us to cut off the mains supply when a safe level of water is reached in the tank. When somebody has a bath or uses a lot of water the ballcock falls and opens the valve. As the water level rises the ballcock also rises and shuts off the supply.

The whole device uses simple levers to produce a sliding movement.

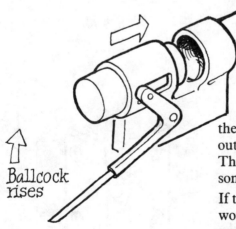

Mains in

Ballcock rises

Overflow System

This is a back-up system. If all else fails, the overflow pipe will drain excess water away out of the building through a pipe in the wall. The water splashing out of this pipe shows that something is wrong.

If this was the only system of control then it would be very wasteful. To avoid wastage of water we use the ballcock to control the flow of water automatically.

Control

Open . . .

Open doors can be very dangerous if there is a fire. This is one of the reasons why we are encouraged to shut all doors at night. The closed door allows the fire to be contained for vital minutes. However, in public buildings such as schools, hospitals and offices, a whole range of control systems are used to shut doors.

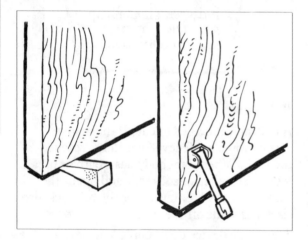

Keeping It Open

A door is something that we use many times a day but have you noticed all the mechanisms needed to keep it open? A simple wedge of rubber or wood on the floor can hold a door open, or a spring lever can do the same job. It just folds out of the way when not needed.

Task 1

Can you explain other methods of keeping doors open?

Keeping It Closed

Some ingenious devices have been designed to keep doors shut yet still allow easy opening. They are also difficult to observe.

Rising Butt/Using a Wedge

The rising butt hinge is a simple wedge twisted around to form a helix. The bottom half of the hinge is fixed to the frame and the upper part to the door. The door can be dropped on to the hinge and the door will rotate, rising and falling as it opens and shuts. The closing action is automatic and relies on the weight of the door.

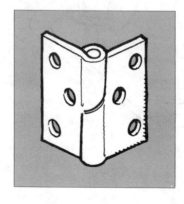
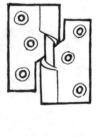

... and Shut

Spring-loaded Closers

Springs can store energy, and it is this energy which we use to close doors automatically. The two methods shown use two types of springs. They are *torsion* and *tension* springs.

A **torsion spring** is a spring which resists twisting.

A **tension spring** is a spring which resists pulling apart.

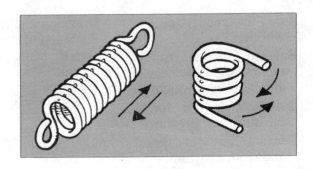

A door-closer is hidden in the door. The chain is attached to a powerful tension spring. When the door is opened the spring is pulled apart. If the door is left open the spring will pull the door shut.

Aluminium section doors have a slim frame so it is very difficult to insert a spring. It is done, however, by using a torsion spring at the top of the opening door. The spring is very powerful and it also acts as the hinge.

Torsion spring inside twists hinge

Aluminium door frame

Task 2

Buses and coaches have doors that are operated by the driver using remote control. There is a hiss of air as they are opened and closed. Can you identify the control system used and can you see what makes the doors move?

Axle A bar connecting wheels.

Balance Two sides equal; a method used for checking and measuring weight.

Barometer A device for measuring air pressure.

Bearings Sleeve to support and reduce friction between two surfaces.

Plain bearings Tube-like sleeve usually made of bronze or plastic.

Ball roller bearings Bearings designed to carry heavy loads at high speeds using either ball-bearings or small rollers.

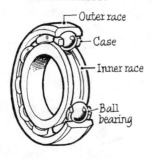

Bimetallic strip A strip made of two metals with a different rate of thermal expansion. Usually seen in temperature-sensing devices. The strip provides the input motion.

Brakes A method of using friction to stop movement. Calliper brakes – seen on bicycles; drum brakes – these may be operated by a cable or hydraulics.

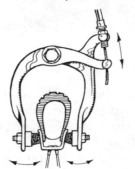

Cam A device for changing a rotary motion into a reciprocating motion (backwards and forwards).

Clutch A device that allows a machine to be disconnected from its drive. Two plates are pressed together by springs and the friction between the plates connects the drive.

Contraction In the process of cooling down, materials tend to become slightly reduced in size.

Counterbalance A known weight arranged to balance out loads – as in a lift system.

Crank A turning handle that is made longer to help make the turning easier, e.g. mincer, bicycle.

Dynamo A device for changing mechanical energy into electrical energy. On a bicycle the rotation of the wheel through friction is a power source for a light.

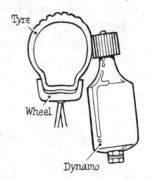

Equilibrium A state of balance. Both sides are equal.

Expansion When materials are heated they tend to become slightly larger.

Friction A force created by rubbing two objects together, thus resisting movement between them.

Gears Toothed wheels which mesh together, used to transmit rotary motion from one shaft to another without slippage.

Spur gear A simple gear like a wheel with teeth round its rim.

Worm-gear Like a screw-thread, with teeth cut along the shaft. This gear is used to change the axis of rotation and to make large reductions in speed from one shaft to another.

Bevel gear A gear with teeth set at an angle so that the direction of motion can be changed.

Rack and pinion A rack is a straight row of gear teeth. The pinion is a small spur gear that pulls the rack backwards and forwards.

Facecut gear The teeth of the gear are cut round the flat surface of a disc, all pointing towards the centre.

Gear ratio The relationship between the input gear and the output gear.

Levers A simple machine used in many household tools. There are three types, all of which have an applied effort, a fulcrum or pivot, and a load.

First class lever The fulcrum is in the middle and the load is on the other side.

Second class lever The effort and load are on the same side of the fulcrum, with the load nearest to the fulcrum e.g. a wheelbarrow.

Third class lever The effort and load are on the same side of the fulcrum, with the effort nearest to the fulcrum e.g. a pair of tweezers.

Linkages Two or more levers or connecting rods fitted together to produce a desired movement.

Lubrication Fluids, such as oil, placed between moving surfaces for ease of movement.

Movement There are several types of movement which can be produced by mechanical means:

Linear Movement in a straight line and in one direction.

Reciprocating Movement backwards and forwards in a straight line.

Oscillating A swinging movement back and forth, like a pendulum.

Rotary A circular movement.

Nut and bolt A bolt has parallel sides with an external thread cut along it. A nut has an internal thread and fits on to a bolt. Often used as pivots when making linkage devices.

Pawl and ratchet The ratchet is a toothed wheel, like a gear. The pawl rests between the teeth and only allows the ratchet to turn one way. For a double-pawl regulated movement, see the clock.

Pulley and belt A wheel with a groove cut around its circumference into which a belt fits.

Mini-Dictionary

Screw-thread A sort of inclined plane. Cut a piece of paper into a right-angled triangle, wrap the paper around a pencil and one edge will make a spiral like a screw-thread. The distance between one point on the spiral and the next point along is called the pitch of the thread.

Spring A thin, coiled piece of metal – a device for storing energy. There can be many types of springs:

> *Tension spring* A spring which resists pulling apart.

Compression spring A spring which resists pushing together.

Torsion spring A spring which resists twisting.

Sprocket and chain On a bicycle, the chain fits over teeth on the sprocket to make a non-slip drive.

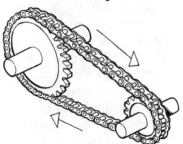

Toothed belt and pulley Similar to pulley and belt but designed to overcome slipping and avoid noise.

Wheel A circular disc; it may be solid or spoked. Most useful when an axle is attached through the centre.

Index